Contents

		Pages
	Safety	4 - 7
	Healthy Eating	8 - 13
	Oral Hygiene	14 - 17
	Keeping Active	18 - 21
	Early Learning	22 - 25
	Contacts	26

Safety

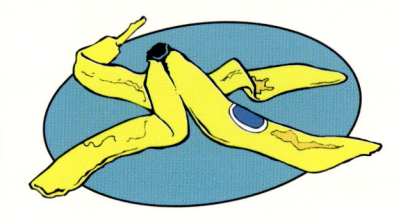

Beware - Children love to explore. Accidents can happen in seconds. Don't be caught out!

- Make sure that your child cannot open any outside door. Keep the keys near the doors in case of fire, but out of reach of your child.

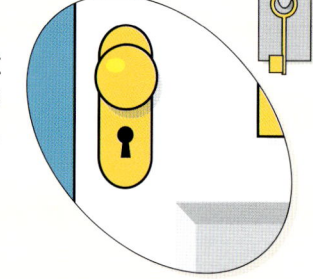

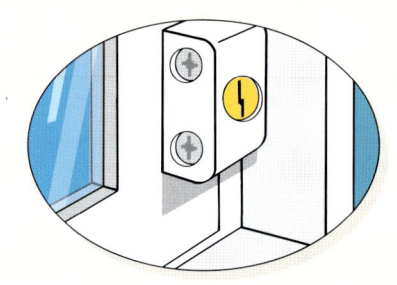

- Fit window locks so that windows cannot be opened wide enough to fall from.

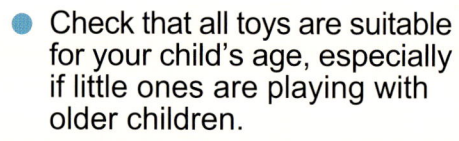

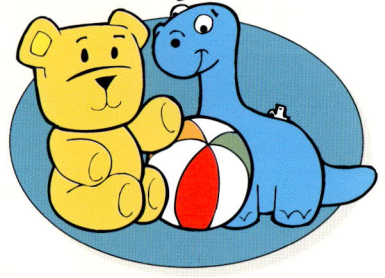

- Check that all toys are suitable for your child's age, especially if little ones are playing with older children.

- Keep toys clean and throw broken toys away.

Safety

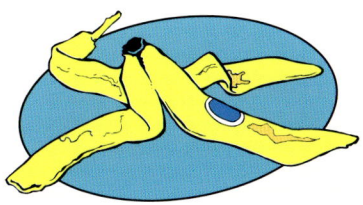

- Use back rings on a cooker and turn pan handles away from the edges of the cooker or work surface.
  Better still fit a cooker guard.

- Don't leave flexes dangling.

- Keep sharp knives out of reach.

- Teach children not to play in the kitchen or the bathroom.
  Check for toys that you might trip over.

Safety

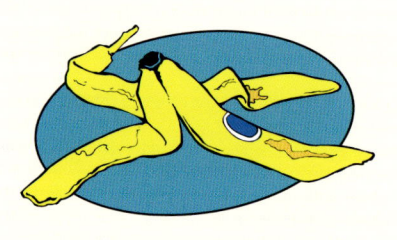

OUT & ABOUT

- Never let your child play out alone.

- Always keep hold of your child when you are out together.

- Use a child car seat, ideally in the back of the car, for ALL journeys.

Safety

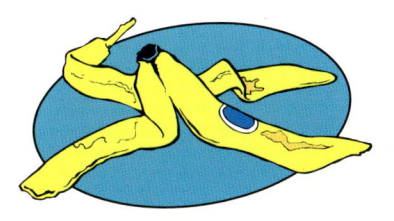

- Your child will be keen to explore other places that you visit.

Don't forget that homes without young children are likely to have lots of dangerous things within easy reach of your child.

Healthy Eating

Every day your child needs a balanced and varied diet:

- **Some milk or dairy products**
  Milk is important for young children to provide energy for growth and calcium for strong teeth and bones.
  Skimmed milk is not suitable for children under five.

- **Some protein foods**
  Your child needs at least one portion of protein food each day for growth and development.

- **Not so many fatty or sugary foods**
  Fatty and sugary foods should be limited at all ages to keep your family healthy. Consider these foods as extras once your child has eaten well from other food groups.

Healthy Eating

- **Plenty of bread, cereal, rice, pasta and potatoes**
  Starchy foods provide energy, various nutrients and some fibre. They are an important part of your child's diet, but can be very filling, so make sure that small tummies have room for other foods as well.
  It is good to give a variety of starchy foods, but do not give only wholemeal grain foods to under fives.

- **Lots of fruit and vegetables**
  Fruit and vegetables contain lots of vitamins, minerals and fibre. Encourage your child to have five different portions of fruit and vegetables every day.

Healthy Eating

● Some important things to remember when preparing food for your child:

FAT
Young children need the concentrated energy provided by foods such as full fat milk, yogurt, cheese and oily fish.
BUT fatty foods such as crisps, chips, cakes, biscuits and fried foods should be limited.

SALT
Limit the amount of salty foods. Don't add salt to your cooking.

SUGAR
Fruit and vegetables contain sugar, but in a form that doesn't damage teeth. Discourage giving sugar-coated cereal or adding sugar to plain cereals or milk.

Healthy Eating

IRON
Iron is essential for your child's physical and mental development. Iron can come from animal foods or plant foods.

● Good sources of iron (animal foods)

- Beef, pork, lamb or liver
- Canned sardines, pilchards, mackerel or tuna.

The iron in animal foods is easier for the body to absorb.

● Good sources of iron (plant food)

- Fortified breakfast cereals
- Dark green vegetables
- Breads
- Beans, peas and lentils
- Dried fruits such as raisins and apricots.

If your child does not eat animal foods, make sure that he/she eats plenty of iron rich plant foods.

Healthy Eating

- Ensure that your toddler always washes his/her hands before eating and after using the toilet.

- Eating together as a family is the best way to encourage good eating habits.

Healthy Eating

Toddlers can often be very fussy about the food that they eat. Try these top tips to encourage good eating habits:

- Give small portions. You can always offer more if your child is still hungry.

- If your child refuses food, don't force-feed him/her or get angry. Remove the food, but don't allow your child to fill up with biscuits or crisps instead.

- Limit in-between meal snacks so that your child is hungry at meal times.

- Don't let your child fill up on drink just before a meal.

- Show by example - children like to copy their parents.

Oral Hygiene

- Brush your child's teeth every morning and every night before bed.

- Use a small pea-sized blob of family toothpaste.

- Encourage your child to have a go at brushing. Give praise for brushing all the teeth carefully and spitting out.

- Young children like to copy adults - let them see you brushing.

Oral Hygiene

- Take your child to the dentist for a check-up every 6 months.

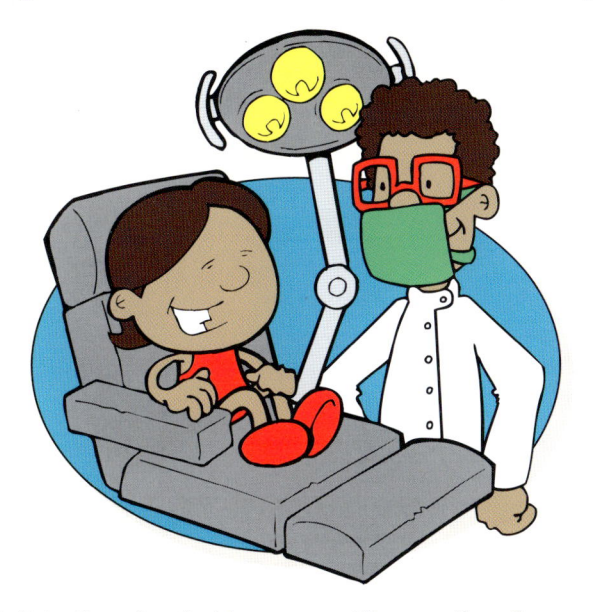

- A visit to the dentist is an exciting outing for your child. He/she will feel very special sitting in the big chair and talking to the dentist.

  - Stop using all dummies and bottles.

Oral Hygiene

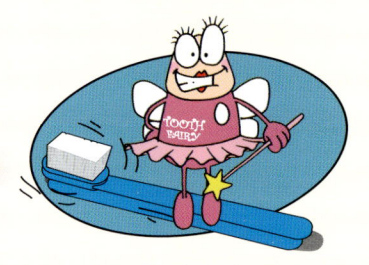

- Limit how often your child has sugary drinks. The number of times that teeth come into contact with sugars is as important as the amount of sugar that is eaten.

doughnuts

sultanas

ice-cream

cola

cake

apple juice

biscuits

- Try to keep sweet foods and drinks for mealtimes, or for after-meal treats when they do less harm to teeth.

Oral Hygiene

- Choose only sugar-free foods and drinks for between-meal snacks.

carrot sticks

milk

apple

celery

natural yogurt

water

bread

orange

Keeping Active

Enjoy walks together:

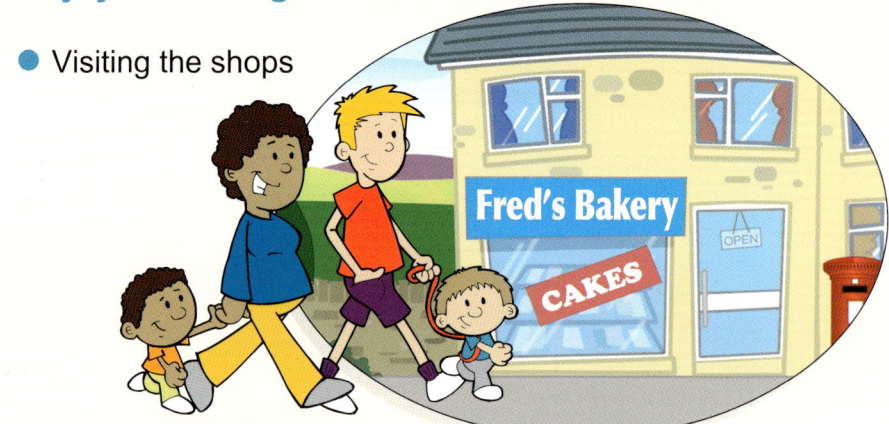

- Visiting the shops

- Splashing in puddles

- Kicking autumn leaves.

Keeping Active

- Make a splash at your local pool.

- Learn to climb safely.

Keeping Active

Your child will love to be active with you:

- Dance
- Hop
- Skip

Keeping Active

- Jump
- Play ball
- Have fun together.

Early Learning

Children love to learn and you are their most important teacher.

DO

- Join in with your child's play.

"I'm just putting the rubbish in the bin."

- Talk to your child about everyday routines.

"Bin, big bin Mummy."

"Yes the wheelie bin is very big because it needs to hold all our rubbish."

- Always respond in some way when your child says something.

Early Learning

DO

- Give your child the chance to listen carefully.

Listen, can you hear the clock?

Bong! Bong!

Bong, bong. Listen, clo... clock.

- Listen carefully to your child and give him/her the chance to practise words.

- Limit TV time.

- When your child watches TV try to watch with him/her so that you can talk about what you have seen.

- Only allow your child to watch what is suitable for his/her age.

Early Learning

DO

That giraffe is very tall isn't he?

- Share books. Talking about the pictures together is a great way for your child to learn lots of new words and phrases.

- Encourage your child to share toys and take turns when playing games.

- Find out about playgroups in your area.

Early Learning

DO

- **Explain WHY.**
  If your child misbehaves don't just say 'NO' - explain why.

No you can't run ahead because the shopping centre is very busy. You must hold mummy's hand so that you don't get lost.

WAAAAH!

REMEMBER - Children learn by example.
Your child will copy what you do.

Contacts

In case of an accident, emergency or just advice these are some useful numbers to ring for information and help.

NHS Direct 0845 4647 (England & Wales)

Your call will automatically be put through to your nearest centre and will be charged at local rates (may be more from a mobile).

www.nhsdirect.nhs.uk   www.nhsdirect.wales.nhs.uk

NHS24 (Scotland) 08454 24 24 24 www.nhs24.com

Your local Health Visitor can be contacted via your GP practice.

Add your GP's number here

Your local Fire Service can be contacted for advice on fire prevention.

Child Accident Prevention Trust (CAPT) 020 7608 3828
A charity committed to reducing childhood injury.
www.capt.org.uk

First Aid Courses
British Red Cross 0844 871 800
St John Ambulance 0870 010 4950

Useful numbers in your area: